Mohamed Ali Bouker

Mean-shift et histogrammes de couleurs

Mohamed Ali Bouker

Mean-shift et histogrammes de couleurs

couleurs

Recherche d'images par le contenu

Presses Académiques Francophones

Impressum / Mentions légales
Bibliografische Information der Deutschen Nationalbibliothek: Die Deutsche Nationalbibliothek verzeichnet diese Publikation in der Deutschen Nationalbibliografie; detaillierte bibliografische Daten sind im Internet über http://dnb.d-nb.de abrufbar. Alle in diesem Buch genannten Marken und Produktnamen unterliegen warenzeichen-, marken- oder patentrechtlichem Schutz bzw. sind Warenzeichen oder eingetragene Warenzeichen der jeweiligen Inhaber. Die Wiedergabe von Marken, Produktnamen, Gebrauchsnamen, Handelsnamen, Warenbezeichnungen u.s.w. in diesem Werk berechtigt auch ohne besondere Kennzeichnung nicht zu der Annahme, dass solche Namen im Sinne der Warenzeichen- und Markenschutzgesetzgebung als frei zu betrachten wären und daher von jedermann benutzt werden dürften.

Information bibliographique publiée par la Deutsche Nationalbibliothek: La Deutsche Nationalbibliothek inscrit cette publication à la Deutsche Nationalbibliografie; des données bibliographiques détaillées sont disponibles sur internet à l'adresse http://dnb.d-nb.de. Toutes marques et noms de produits mentionnés dans ce livre demeurent sous la protection des marques, des marques déposées et des brevets, et sont des marques ou des marques déposées de leurs détenteurs respectifs. L'utilisation des marques, noms de produits, noms communs, noms commerciaux, descriptions de produits, etc, même sans qu'ils soient mentionnés de façon particulière dans ce livre ne signifie en aucune façon que ces noms peuvent être utilisés sans restriction à l'égard de la législation pour la protection des marques et des marques déposées et pourraient donc être utilisés par quiconque.

Coverbild / Photo de couverture: www.ingimage.com

Verlag / Editeur:
Presses Académiques Francophones
ist ein Imprint der / est une marque déposée de
AV Akademikerverlag GmbH & Co. KG
Heinrich-Böcking-Str. 6-8, 66121 Saarbrücken, Deutschland / Allemagne
Email: info@presses-academiques.com

Herstellung: siehe letzte Seite /
Impression: voir la dernière page
ISBN: 978-3-8381-7567-6

RECHERCHE D'IMAGES PAR LE CONTENU BASÉE SUR MEAN-SHIFT ET
HISTOGRAMMES DE COULEURS

THÈSE PRÉSENTÉE À LA FACULTÉ DES ÉTUDES SUPÉRIEURES ET DE
LA RECHERCHE EN VUE DE L'OBTENTION DE LA MAÎTRISE ÈS
SCIENCES EN INFORMATIQUE

MOHAMED ALI BOUKER

DÉPARTEMENT D'INFORMATIQUE
FACULTÉ DES SCIENCES
UNIVERSITÉ DE MONCTON
CAMPUS DE MONCTON

AVRIL 2012

COMPOSITION DU JURY

Président du jury

Jalal Almhana
Dr. / Prof. Université de Moncton, Moncton

Examinateur externe

Nabil Belacel
Agent de recherche senior, CNRC Moncton

Examinateur interne

Mustapha Kardouchi
Dr. / Prof. Université de Moncton, Moncton

Directeur de thèse

Éric Hervet
Dr. / Prof. Université de Moncton, Moncton

REMERCIEMENTS

Pour commencer, je tiens à exprimer ma profonde gratitude au Prof. Éric Hervet, mon directeur de thèse, qui m'a permis de m'engager dans cette spécialité. Qu'il soit vivement remercié pour l'encadrement qu'il m'a offert tout au long de ma maîtrise, pour tout le temps qu'il m'a accordé et pour les soutiens financiers et moraux dont j'ai bénéficié auprès de lui.

Je tiens également à dire un grand merci à chaque membre du jury, le Prof. Mustapha Kardouchi, le Prof. Nabil Belacel qui ont eu l'amabilité d'examiner ce travail de recherche ainsi qu'au président de jury, le Prof. Jalal Almhana.

Il m'est très agréable d'exprimer aussi ma reconnaissance à mes enseignantes et enseignants, qui ont joué un rôle fondamental dans ma formation. Que mes professeures et professeurs au Département d'informatique de l'Université de Moncton trouvent ici l'expression de ma gratitude infinie pour leur disponibilité perpétuelle et pour avoir enrichi ma réflexion.

LISTE DES TABLEAUX

Table I-1. The parameter p, the number of colors in each packet, and the number of color packets...7

Table I-2. Recall / Precision ratios for the ten images of figure 1....................................12

Table I-3. Comparison Chart...13

Table II-1. The parameter p, the number of colors in each packet, and the number of color packets...19

Table II-2. Confusion Matrix (in percentages) for the WHMSGM method.................24

LISTE DES FIGURES

Figure I-1.Ten images from the COIL database 11

Figure I-2.Recall / Precision ratios for four COIL images...........................13

Figure II-1. A few images from Corel-1000...23

Figure II-2. Reference images 25

Figure II-3. Intra-class ordering for the reference images shown in figure 2....................27

TABLE DES MATIÈRES

RÉSUMÉ IX

RÉSUMÉ (VERSION ANGLAISE) X

AVANT-PROPOS XI

INTRODUCTION GÉNÉRALE 1

1   Problématique 2

2   Objectifs 2

CHAPITRE I
RECHERCHE D'IMAGES BASÉE SUR LA CLASSIFICATION PAR MEAN-
SHIFT EN UTILISANT LES DESCRIPTEURS DE COULEURS...........3

I.1   Introduction.. 4

I.2   Indexation de couleur 5

    I.2.1   Histogrammes de couleurs pondérés.............................. 5

    I.2.2   Les paquets de couleurs 6

I.3   La classification par Mean-Shift.. 8

    I.3.1   Mean-Shift...8

    I.3.2   Mesure de similarité... 9

I.4   Algorithme général.. 10

I.5   Résultat.. 10

    I.5.1   Base de données et recherche précédente 10

    I.5.2   Expériences et résultats... 12

I.6   Conclusion...14

CHAPITRE II
RECHERCHE D'IMAGES PAR LE CONTENU EN UTILISANT MEAN-SHIFT
ET LES MELANGES DE GAUSSIENNES BASES SUR LES HISTOGRAMMES
DE COULEURS..15

II.1 Introduction.. 16

II.2 Indexation de couleur 18

    II.2.1 Histogrammes de couleurs pondérés 18

    II.2.2 Paquets de couleurs 19

II.3 Mean-Shift et Mélange de Gaussiennes 20

    II.3.1 Mean-Shift 20

    II.3.2 Mélange de Gaussiennes 21

II.4 Résultats et expérimentations 22

    II.4.1 Base de données d'images 22

    II.4.2 Matrice de confusion 24

    II.4.3 Ordonnancement intra-classe 25

II.5 Conclusion 28

CONCLUSION GÉNÉRALE 29

BIBLIOGRAPHIE 31

TABLE OF CONTENTS

ABSTRACT (FRENCH VERSION) IX

ABSTRACT X

FOREWORD XI

GENERAL INTRODUCTION 1

1   Problem 2

2   Objectives 2

CHAPTER I

IMAGE RETRIEVAL BASED ON MEAN-SHIFT CLUSTERING USING COLOR DESCRIPTOR 3

I.1 Introduction 4

I.2 Color indexing 5

     I.2.1   Weighted color histograms 5

     I.2.2   Color Packets 6

I.3 Mean-Shift Clustering 8

     I.3.1   Mean-Shift 8

     I.3.2   Similarity measure 9

I.4 General algorithm 10

I.5 Results 10

     I.5.1   Database and previous research 10

     I.5.2   Experiments and results 12

I.6 Conclusion 14

CHAPTER II

RETRIEVAL OF IMAGES USING MEAN-SHIFT AND GAUSSIAN MIXTURES BASED ON WEIGHTED COLOR HISTOGRAMS 15

II.1 Introduction 16

II.2 Color indexing 18

     II.2.1 Weighted Color Histograms 18

II.2.2 Color packets... 19

II.3 Mean-Shift and Gaussian Mixtures 20

II.3.1 Mean-Shift 20

II.3.2 Gaussian Mixtures... 21

II.4 Results and experiments 22

II.4.1 Image database.. 22

II.4.2 Confusion matrix... 24

II.4.3 Intra-class ordering 25

II.5 Conclusion 28

GENERAL CONCLUSION... **29**

REFERENCES... **31**

RÉSUMÉ

Le « Mean-Shift » est une technique d'analyse non paramétrique qui peut être appliquée à la classification et au traitement d'images. Cette procédure a été présentée la première fois par Fukunaga et Hostetler en 1975. C'est une procédure de localisation des maxima d'une fonction de densité de données discrètes.

Elle est utile pour détecter les modes de cette fonction de densité. Il s'agit d'une méthode itérative qui nécessite comme point de départ une estimation initiale x. Soit une fonction noyau $K(xi - x)$ donnée. Cette fonction détermine le poids des points à proximité de la réestimation de la moyenne. Typiquement, nous utilisons un noyau Gaussien sur la distance à l'estimation actuelle. La moyenne pondérée de la densité dans la fenêtre est déterminée par K.

Cet algorithme peut être utilisé pour le suivi visuel. Une technique simple serait par exemple de créer une carte de confiance d'une image provenant d'une séquence, basée sur l'histogramme de couleur d'un objet donné d'une image précédente dans la séquence, et d'utiliser Mean-Shift pour trouver le pic de la carte de la confiance à proximité de l'ancienne position de l'objet.

Dans ce projet nous allons faire un suivi de n classes d'une image de référence prise dans une base d'images et tenter de la retrouver, parmi les autres images de la base, toutes celles possédant des classes similaires à celles de l'image de référence.

Si n vaut 2, cela signifie que le suivi des classes se fait à partir de deux classes de couleurs pour l'image de référence et pour chacune des autres images de la base. Pour effectuer le suivi des classes, deux techniques robustes souvent utilisées en traitement d'images sont utilisées dans notre approche : l'algorithme du Mean-Shift et les modèles de mélanges de gaussiennes.

Mots-clés: Mean-Shift, Recherche d'images par le contenu, Classification d'images, Mélange de gaussiennes.

ABSTRACT

Mean-Shift is a non parametric analysis technique which can be applied to image processing and classification. This procedure has been presented first by Fukunaga and Hostetler in 1975. It is aimed at localizing the maxima of a density function of discrete data.

It is used to detect the modes of the density function. It is an iterative method, using as a start point an initial estimation x. Let us note $K(xi - x)$ a given kernel function. This function gives the weights of the points close to the re-estimation of the mean. Typically, a Gaussian kernel is used on the distance to the current estimation. The weighted mean of the density inside a window is given by K.

This algorithm can be used for visual tracking. A simple technique would consist for example in creating a confidence map of a given image from a sequence, based on the color histogram of a specific object from a previous image, and use Mean-Shift to find the peak of the confidence map the closest to the previous position of the object.

In this project, we perform the tracking of n classes of a given, reference image taken from an image database, and we try to find other images in this database that have the most similar classes to the reference image.

If n equals 2, this means the tracking takes into account 2 color classes for the reference image and every other image in the database. To perform the tracking, two robust techniques often used in image processing will help us classifying and tracking color classes: Mean-Shift and Gaussian Mixtures.

Key words: Mean-Shift, Content Based Image Search, Image Classification, Gaussian Mixtures.

AVANT-PROPOS

Cette thèse de maîtrise intitulée « Extraction et reconnaissance de formes dans des bases d'images et recherche par similarité » résume mes travaux dans le cadre de mon projet de recherche pour l'obtention du diplôme de Maîtrise ès sciences en informatique. Cette thèse comprend deux chapitres dont chacun traite un problème typique du domaine de la recherche d'image par le contenu (*image retrieval*). Le premier chapitre est constitué d'un article qui a déjà été publié dans une conférence internationale, et le deuxième chapitre est un article soumis à une autre conférence internationale. Ces deux articles présentent des points communs puisqu'ils traitent du même sujet, cependant, chaque chapitre peut être lu de façon indépendante.

Les deux chapitres sont rédigés dans la langue anglaise, tout en respectant les exigences de la Faculté des Études Supérieures et de la Recherche concernant le format, Cependant, j'ai pris soin de rédiger l'introduction et la conclusion en langue française.

Mon premier article s'intitule « *Image Retrieval based on Mean-Shift Clustering using Color Descriptor* ». Il traite du problème d'indexation d'images et de la recherche basée sur le contenu. Ce travail a été soumis à « *ISSPA 2012 the International Conference on Information Science, Internet Signal Processing and their Applications (sponsored by IEEE)* » qui se déroulera en juillet 2012 à Montréal, Québec, Canada.

Le deuxième article est une extension du premier travail. L'article porte le titre « *Retrieval of images using Mean-Shift and Gaussian Mixtures based on Weighted Color Histograms* » et a été présenté le 28 décembre 2011 à « *SITIS 2011: the International Conference on Signal Image Technology and Internet Based Systems (sponsored by IEEE)* » à Dijon, en France.

Une recherche bibliographique sur l'indexation d'images par le contenu m'a amené à explorer deux familles de méthodes : les méthodes par descripteurs globaux et celles par caractéristiques locales. Cette revue de littérature m'a donné la chance de me familiariser avec plusieurs approches efficaces, en particulier l'application du modèle « Mean-Shift » qui a fait l'objet de plusieurs recherches récentes. Une étude approfondie de cette approche m'a permis de découvrir les limites des travaux existants sur ce sujet et de proposer des idées d'améliorations. Les résultats obtenus suite à mes travaux m'ont permis de rédiger les articles cités ci-dessus. En effet, les résultats expérimentaux ont confirmé mes hypothèses en démontrant l'efficacité de la méthode proposée.

Cette étude approfondie a été encadrée par le Prof. Éric Hervet (mon directeur de thèse). Mon directeur m'a guidé tout au long de la réalisation de ma thèse en m'aidant depuis la définition du sujet jusqu'à la publication des résultats.

Introduction générale

La diversité et l'augmentation du nombre de bases d'images numériques et leur évolution rapide ces dernières années ont accru de façon impressionnante la capacité de stockage physique. C'est pourquoi il est devenu primordial pour beaucoup de personnes et d'organismes de disposer de techniques performantes et de méthodes intelligentes de traitement d'images afin d'accéder et de gérer de manière plus efficace les grandes quantités d'images numériques disponibles.

Notre travail s'intéresse spécialement à la recherche d'images par le contenu et à la classification. La recherche par le contenu consiste à trouver dans une base d'images, les images les plus similaires à une image requête, alors que la classification consiste à classifier chaque image dans sa catégorie correspondante. Ce travail est depuis plusieurs années le centre d'intérêt de nombreuses recherches et beaucoup de temps et d'énergie sont investis pour développer et améliorer ce domaine. Malgré cela, on remarque que les résultats obtenus jusqu'à date ne sont pas concluants. Nous avons adapté la méthode d'analyse statistique « Mean-Shift » à une recherche de similarité entre une image requête et des images d'une base. Cette méthode prend en considération la signature couleur de l'image requête en la comparant avec les autres images de la base. Ensuite, nous utilisons une mesure de ressemblance basée sur le coefficient de Bhattacharyya pour calculer le pourcentage de similarité entre l'image requête et chaque autre image de la base. Ainsi nous pouvons procéder à une recherche des images de la base les plus ressemblantes à l'image requête, ou bien opter pour une classification des images selon des critères prédéfinis.

Plutôt que de compter sur les métadonnées introduites par des personnes – telles que les titres et les mots-clés – pour décrire des images et leurs catégories, la recherche par le contenu et la classification consistent à analyser et à extraire automatiquement des caractéristiques visuelles à partir des pixels des images pour procéder à leur indexation. Cependant, un problème difficile à résoudre est celui de la différence entre une image constituée de pixels et les objets de la vie réelle qu'elle représente : comment traduire la similarité sémantique entre images en une similarité visuelle?

1. Problématique

Les descripteurs globaux ont été les premiers utilisés dans ce domaine, tels que l'histogramme de couleurs [1], la co-occurrence de couleurs [2] et les filtres de Gabor [3]. Malgré leurs bonnes performances, elles restent cependant limitées.

« Mean-Shift » est une méthode d'analyse statistique par caractéristiques globales. L'indexation d'une base d'images par cette approche consiste dans l'extraction des caractéristiques globales de toute la collection pour pouvoir construire un descripteur visuel de chaque image formé par des motifs globaux. Ensuite, un histogramme est construit pour chaque image. Enfin, une similarité est mesurée entre la signature d'une image requête et une autre image pour calculer le pourcentage de ressemblance entres ces deux images.

Le modèle utilisé est très efficace et répond à la fois au besoin de la recherche des images et de la classification. Cependant, on doit connaître à priori le nombre de classes à fournir au modèle, ce qui rend la méthode semi-automatique. Généralement le nombre de classes ne devrait pas dépasser trois pour un temps d'exécution raisonnable.

2. Objectifs

L'objectif de cette recherche est d'étudier en profondeur l'approche « Mean-Shift » pour l'indexation d'images et son application à la recherche par le contenu et à la classification. Ce travail nous permettra d'améliorer les recherches précédentes, de valider l'implémentation proposée et de la comparer aux autres méthodes dans le domaine. Le but est d'optimiser les performances de la recherche d'images par le contenu et de la classification sans toutefois la rendre trop complexe et coûteuse en temps d'exécution.

CHAPITRE I

IMAGE RETRIEVAL BASED ON MEAN-SHIFT CLUSTERING USING COLOR DESCRIPTOR

RECHERCHE D'IMAGES BASÉE SUR LA CLASSIFICATION PAR MEAN-SHIFT EN UTILISANT LES DESCRIPTEURS DE COULEURS

Mohamed Ali Bouker, Eric Hervet

Texte original de l'article soumis le 23 janvier 2012 à la conférence « *ISSPA 2012: the International Conference on Information Science, Internet Signal Processing and their Applications (sponsored by IEEE)* ».

Abstract

Content-based indexing of images extracts visual information from digital images (such as pixels, colors, objects, shapes, etc.), and can be performed automatically and quickly by computers. This work focuses on indexing color distributions of objects in images. A statistical algorithm called Mean-Shift Clustering is used to modelize the color distributions of objects in images as 2-dimensional elliptical Gaussian kernels. The experiments have been performed on the COIL database from Columbia University and the results show that the proposed method compares well to other content-based retrieval methods

Index Terms: Content-Based Image Retrieval; Mean-Shift; Color Histograms; Recall/Precision.

I.1 Introduction

The search for images in databases is usually performed by two ways: by keywords or by visual content. In some cases these two approaches can be combined to improve the performance of image retrieval. The keywords are used once as an initial criterion for indexing, and subsequently as a search criterion in a database of images previously indexed. The keywords act as a passkey to a given content (one or more texts, one or more images, etc.).

For an efficient search, the keywords should be cautiously selected for their relevance to the content of the images, in order to establish a meaningful correspondence between keywords and visual content. The main disadvantage of keyword indexing is its cost in case of large databases, and its subjectivity.

Image search by content, also called image query by content, is based on a previous, automatic characterization of visual features such as shapes, edges, colors, textures, feature points, etc., of a whole database of images. This first step is called visual indexing. A second step consists in extracting the same visual information from a specific, target image, and comparing it to the indexed database in order to possibly find similar images in it. To the purpose of indexing, analytical, digital image processing techniques are used, capable of extracting visual information in large databases in a reasonable time. The advantage of visual content indexing is that it can be fully automated, regardless of the size of the image database, and is not dependent on the subjectivity of keyword indexing. Many approaches for automatic indexing and search of images by content have already been explored. Swain and Ballard were the first to use color histograms to describe images [4].

Other authors have introduced different features such as texture [5], color moments [6] or SIFT points (*Scale Invariant Features Transform*) [7,8]. These descriptors achieve and efficient retrieval in most cases, but their accuracy usually reaches a limit due for example to their lack of image rotation, translation, or scale invariance, all features that are usually well handled by color histograms. A recent approach consists in adapting a well-known statistical method, called Mean-Shift [9,10], to the domain of image processing, in order to characterize both globally and locally the distribution of colors in images. For example, Mean-Shift is used successfully in the tracking of objects in videos or sequences of similar images. We use it as a basis to adapt Mean-Shift to the indexing and the searching of images in large databases by visual content based on colors.

The second section of this paper explains the principle of image indexing by weighted color histograms. The third section presents the Mean-Shift Clustering analysis and its application to the modelization of objects in sets of images. This step is necessary to improve the similarity (or dissimilarity) of objects in large databases of images representing various scenes or objects. The fourth section summarizes the whole algorithm used to implement our method. The fifth section presents the results of our work, and finally the sixth section concludes the paper. In the rest of the paper, we abbreviate our approach as MSCA for: "Mean-Shift Clustering Analysis".

I.2   Color indexing

I.2.1   Weighted color histograms

Image indexing by color histograms consists in computing the statistical distribution of the colors in an image. For an image of size $M \times N$ pixels, the histogram $h(c)$ is formerly defined as:

$$h(c) = \frac{1}{MN} \sum_{i=0}^{M-1} \sum_{j=0}^{N-1} \delta(f(i,j) - c) \forall c \in C \tag{1}$$

Where $f(i,j)$ is the color of the image f at pixel (i,j), c is a color varying in a colorset C, and δ is the Kronecker function: ($\delta(x-y)=1$ if x equals y, 0 otherwise).

However this approach is limited because it does not take into account the spatial distribution of colors inside the image. To overcome this issue, an efficient and simple way consists in weighting the histogram by the local color activity around each pixel [11]. Then (1) becomes:

$$h(c) = \frac{1}{MN} \sum_{i=0}^{M-1} \sum_{j=0}^{N-1} w(i,j) \delta(f(i,j) - c) \quad \forall c \in C \tag{2}$$

where $w(i,j)$ is the coefficient associated to each pixel. A commonly used weighting scheme is based on Laplacian, because it provides good information regarding uniform areas or edges:
$$w(i,j) = \Delta^2(i,j) \tag{3}$$

More generally, weight $w(i,j)$ has to be a statistical measure that takes into account the probability of the current color within its neighborhood. For example the inverse of entropy is commonly used too, since local entropy $E_{ij}(c)$ is null in a uniform neighborhood and maximal where there are no identical colors within a neighborhood:

$$w(i,j) = \frac{1}{E_{ij}(c)} \tag{4}$$

This is the weighting scheme we used in our implementation.

I.2.2   Color packets

Our work deals with databases of color images, where every color pixel is usually coded as a triplet (R,G,B) of values of red, green, and blue. Usually for general images, each color channel is usually composed of 256 bins. This gives a choice of color among a range of $256^3 = 16,777,216$ possible colors. This is the number of colors in the colorset C in (1), (2), and (4). Computing a weighted histogram like in (2) with such a palette would be too much time consuming, especially in case of large databases containing hundreds or thousands of images, and of high resolution images. For example pictures from digital cameras are nowadays commonly over five million pixels. In order to reduce the computing time, the color set is split into color packets. A parameter p controls the number of packets, and thus the number of colors inside each packet. Table 1 shows the parameter p (first column), the number of colors in each packet (second column), and the number of color packets (third column).

Table I-1

THE PARAMETER P, THE NUMBER OF COLORS IN EACH PACKET, AND THE NUMBER OF COLOR PACKETS.

Parameter p	$2^{(p)}$ colors/packet	$2^{(24-p)}$ packets
0	1	16, 777,216
3	8	2, 097,152
6	64	262,144
9	512	32,768
12	4,096	4,096
15	32,768	512
18	262,144	64
21	2, 097,152	8
24	16, 777,216	1

In the indexing phase, (2) can be easily adapted to compute the frequencies $h(p_c)$ of color packets p_c instead of single colors c. The choice of parameter p depends on the compromise we want between computing time and accuracy of indexing. An extreme case would be to consider $p=24$, meaning that the whole colorset is seen as a single packet containing all the colors in the image. It would be the worst case to distinguish between different images but the fastest for computing time. Another extreme case would be to set $p=0$, where a packet contains one single color, yielding maximum accuracy but at the cost of a much higher computing time. In our implementation we set p to 9. The next section explains how the weighted histogram of an image is used to compute 2D Gaussian kernels of color distributions.

I.3   Mean-Shift clustering

I.3.1   Mean-Shift

The Mean-Shift procedure is a non parametric clustering technique analysis which, unlike the well-known K-means clustering approach [12], does not require prior knowledge of the number of clusters, and does not constrain the shape of the clusters.

Given n data points x_i, $i = 1,..,n$ on a d-dimensional space R^d, the multivariate kernel density estimate using a radially symmetric kernel (case of a Gaussian kernel) $K(x)$ is given by:

$$\hat{f}(x) = \frac{1}{nh^d} \sum_{i=1}^{n} K(\frac{x - x_i}{h})$$ (5)

where h represents the radius of the kernel, and K is defined as: $K(x) = c.k\left(\|x\|^2\right)$ where c is a normalization constant which assures $K(x)$ integrates to 1.

The modes of the density function are located at the zeros of the gradient function $\nabla \hat{f}(x) = 0$ with $\nabla \hat{f}(x)$ defined as:

The gradient of the density estimator (5) is

$$\nabla \hat{f}(x) = \frac{2c}{nh^{d+2}} \sum_{i=1}^{n} (x_i - x) g\left(\left\|\frac{x - x_i}{h}\right\|^2\right)$$

$$= \frac{2c}{nh^{d+2}} \left[\sum_{i=1}^{n} g\left(\left\|\frac{x - x_i}{h}\right\|^2\right) \right] \left[\frac{\sum_{i=1}^{n} x_i g\left(\left\|\frac{x - x_i}{h}\right\|^2\right)}{\sum_{i=1}^{n} g\left(\left\|\frac{x - x_i}{h}\right\|^2\right)} - x \right]$$ (6)

where $g(s) = -k'(s)$ denotes the derivative of the selected kernel profile.

The first term is proportional to the density estimate at x, and the second term, called the mean-shift vector, points toward the direction of maximum increase in density and is proportional to the density gradient estimate at point x obtained with kernel K. The mean-shift procedure for a given point x_i is as follows:

1. Compute the Mean-Shift vector $m(x_i^j)$;
2. Translate density estimation window: $x_i^{j+1} = x_i^j + m(x_i^j)$;
3. Iterate steps 1. and 2. until convergence, i.e., $\nabla f(x_i) = 0$.

The method we developed consists in analyzing the colors of a « target image », then building a confidence map by comparison to another image called " target image ". The confidence map is built by comparing the color distributions between the reference and the target images. Especially, we try to detect in the target image the objects characterized by their colors in the reference image, and then measure a similarity or dissimilarity. This is how we have adapted the Mean-Shift method to our purpose. The comparison between two color distributions, technically in our case two weighted color histograms (see Section 2), is performed by a statistical distance commonly called similarity measure (see Section 3.2).

While the Mean-Shift method used in object tracking in videos usually considers only one single class due to real-time computation constraints, i.e. one single 2D Gaussian color distribution characterizing the object to track, our contribution here, taking into account the fact that some objects or scenes can be complex, is to consider several 2D color distributions for a single object, and then measure the similarity between two sets of 2D Gaussian distributions.

I.3.2   Similarity measure

The similarity measure used to compare different color classes modelized as Gaussian distributions is based on Bhattacharyya coefficient [13, 14, 15].

The Bhattacharyya coefficient is used to measure the amount of overlap between two statistical samples, and therefore can be used as a measure of the closeness of the samples.

In order to calculate the Bhattacharyya coefficient, the interval of the values of the two samples is split into a fixed number of partitions, and then the coefficient is defined as:

$$C_B = \sum_{i=1}^{n} \sqrt{n_{a_i} n_{b_i}} \tag{7}$$

where n is the number of partitions, a and b the samples, and n_{a_i}, n_{b_i} the numbers of data from a and b in the i'th partition.

The equation (7) shows that the Bhattacharyya coefficient is larger when a partition has data from both samples, and larger too when a partition has a large overlap of the two samples data within it. The choice of the number of partitions depends on the numbers of members in each sample. Too few partitions will lose accuracy by over-estimating the overlap region, while too many partitions will lose accuracy by creating individual partitions with no members despite being in a surroundingly populated sample space. In our implementation, the number of partitions has been experimentally set to 4 for optimal results.

I.4 General algorithm

- Let the user pick a target image, and delimitate approximatively an object to be characterized with a polygon.
- Compute the weighted color histogram over the polygon area.
- Apply Mean-Shift Clustering to detect and characterize the polygon area by N (chosen by user) Gaussian color distributions.
- For every other image in the database, do:
  - For each previously computed color class, do :
    - Like in Mean-Shift-based tracking [10], search in the current image the optimal position and scale of the area corresponding to the current color class, by varying both the center of the area and its scale.
    - Compute and save the similarity between the color class of current image and the one from initial target image, thanks to the Battacharyya coefficient.
  - End for each color class
- Compute the average similarity over the N color classes, between current and target images.

I.5 Results

I.5.1 Database and previous research

We used the image database named COIL[1] for: Columbia Object Image Library, from Columbia University, to measure the performance of our approach and compare it to other methods in the same field. COIL database contains altogether 7200 images which represent 100 different objects, each object being viewed from 72 different points of view (every 5°). All images have the same size 128x128 pixels. Most of COIL objects contain two predominant colors, a few contain only one or three. This is the reason why the *a priori* number of Gaussian mixtures classes has been set to 2. The background is black in all images and has not been taken into account. Fig. 1 shows ten objects from the COIL database randomly picked up for our experiments.

| Coil1 | Coil2 | Coil3 | Coil4 | Coil5 |

| Coil6 | Coil7 | Coil8 | Coil9 | Coil10 |

Figure I-1. Ten images from the COIL database

Several recent approaches for indexing and retrieval of images by content have also been performed on the COIL database: for example the method "Term Frequency-Inverse Document Frequency (TFX)" [16,17], the method "Term Frequency (TXX)" [18], and the method of "Fuzzy Weighting Scheme" [19].
In the next section, the results obtained by these three approaches on the COIL database are compared to ours.

I.5.2   Experiments and results

To quantitatively measure the performance of our method, we use two criteria

---

[1] Available at: http://www1.cs.columbia.edu/CAVE/software/softlib/coil-100.php

commonly used in the field of content-based image retrieval: the measures of recall and precision. The precision is defined as the ratio of the number of relevant images retrieved by a query, by the total number of images retrieved. The recall is defined as the ratio of the number of images retrieved by a query, by the total number of images belonging to the class of the target object in the whole database. By varying the number of images returned by a query, it is possible to plot curves of the ratio of the recall by the precision as a measure of the performance of a retrieval method. Table 2 shows the values of the precision for 10, 20, 30, 40, 50, 60, and 70 images retrieved from the database. Since every object has the same number of images as the others (72), the recall does not depend on the target image and equals respectively 0.14, 0.28, 0.42, 0.56, 0.70, 0.84, and 0.94. Fig. 2 and Table 2 show the ratio recall / precision of four images out of the ten shown in Fig. 1, and compare our approach "MSCA" to the three others mentioned previously. Table 3 shows that when indexing COIL images using "MSCA", retrieval results are considerably better than those obtained with "TXX", "TFX" and "Fuzzy Weighting".

Table I-2

Recall / Precision ratios for the ten images of figure 1.

gifts	Coil1	Coil 2	Coil 3	Coil 4	Coil 5	Coil 6	Coil 7	Coil 8	Coi9	Coil10	Average
10	1.00	1.00	1.00	1.00	1.00	1.00	1.00	1.00	1.00	1.00	1.00
20	1.00	1.00	1.00	1.00	1.00	1.00	1.00	1.00	1.00	0.75	0.98
30	1.00	1.00	1.00	1.00	1.00	1.00	1.00	1.00	1.00	0.53	0.95
40	0.98	1.00	1.00	1.00	1.00	1.00	1.00	1.00	1.00	0.42	0.94
50	0.92	1.00	1.00	1.00	1.00	1.00	1.00	1.00	1.00	0.38	0.93
60	0.85	0.93	1.00	1.00	1.00	1.00	1.00	1.00	0.98	0.36	0.91
70	0.77	0.88	1.00	0.92	1.00	0.98	0.94	1.00	0.92	0.35	0.88
Average	0.93	0.97	1.00	0.99	1.00	1.00	0.99	1.00	0.99	0.54	

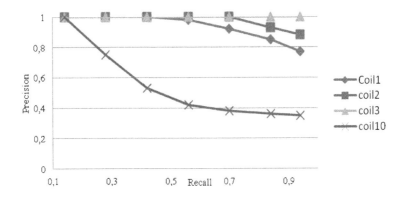

Figure I-1 . Recall / Precision ratios for four COIL images.

Table I-3

Comparison Chart

Approaches	Average precision
TXX	0.72
TFX	0.62
Fuzzy Weighting	0.80
MSCA	0.94

I.6 Conclusion

This paper is a contribution to the domain of image indexing and searching by visual content. It demonstrates the efficiency of a method that combines two statistical analysis methods - Mean-Shift and Gaussian mixtures - in order to model the color distributions of objects in images. The results on a large image database are presented quantitatively and compare favorably to the results obtained by other approaches in the same field and on the same database.

Future work plans to: address more complex image databases; combine color indexing with other visual content criteria, such as contour moments histograms which are currently studied in another master's thesis work in our department; improve computing time by generating fast executable files for example using C or C++ language with optimized compilation and low-level coding of critical functions.

The authors thank the Columbia University for the availability of the COIL database used in this research.

CHAPITRE II

RETRIEVAL OF IMAGES USING MEAN-SHIFT AND GAUSSIAN MIXTURES BASED ON WEIGHTED COLOR HISTOGRAMS

RECHERCHE D'IMAGES PAR LE CONTENU EN UTILISANT MEAN-SHIFT ET LES MELANGES DE GAUSSIENNES BASES SUR LES HISTOGRAMMES DE COULEURS

Mohamed Ali Bouker, Éric Hervet

Texte original de l'article publié le 28 décembre 2011 à la conférence « *SITIS 2011: the International Conference on Signal Image Technology and Internet Based Systems (sponsored by IEEE)* ».

Abstract

The topic of this paper is Content-Based Image Retrieval (CBIR) based on colors as a content image descriptor. The tool we developed to that purpose modelizes the colors of an image as a set of 2D Gaussian distributions based on weighted color histograms. Then, given a reference image proposed by a user, the system can automatically classify the image and provide the user with the most similar images to the reference image in its category. Experiments with Corel-1000 dataset demonstrate that our method outperforms the known implementations

Index Terms: Content-Based Image Retrieval; Image Classification; Color Histograms; Mean-Shift; Gaussian Mixtures.

II.1 Introduction

This paper focuses on Content-Based Image Retrieval (CBIR) using color distribution as a primary visual image descriptor. CBIR has numerous and various public applications as well as professional ones. Among the well-known, public applications, we can think of the image search engines on the internet like Google Image, but their performance are limited in terms of low-level image features. For instance, Most of the image search engines use mainly the name of the image file and the title of the web page containing the image, often providing non relevant results. Automatic image retrieval has become a growing issue these last years. Indeed, the burst of multimedia brought up an important problematic: how to manage the huge amount of digital documents available nowadays. In particular, still images or sequences of images are usually archived and compressed into generalist or specialized databases, often accessible through the internet.

To be able to handle such amounts of data and facilitate their management, it is necessary to develop automatic tools for the indexing and searching images. While text-based retrieval of textual data is well known and used efficiently since the seventies, tools for automatic analysis and interpretation of images often do not match their semantics. Usually two levels of indexing are considered: The first one deal with low-level image features like colors, textures, shapes, etc. The second one rather refers to the semantic description of the image.

Many image descriptors for image indexing have already been explored. Swain and Ballard [20] were the first to use color histograms for image indexing. Some other authors introduced different features like texture [21], colorimetric moments [22], or SIFT (Scale-Invariant Features Transform) points [23,24]. These descriptors provide most of the time an efficient retrieval, but are still limited due for example to their lack of image rotation, translation, or scale invariance. A recent approach consists in applying a statistical analysis method called Mean-Shift [25,26], to the image processing domain by characterizing both locally and globally the color content of images. For example Mean-Shift is used efficiently for object tracking in videos. Here we propose to adapt Mean-Shift to content based image retrieval approach. Given a reference image for which the user wants to retrieve similar images, our procedure is composed of two steps: In the first one, an automatic classification of the reference image is performed, based on weighted color histograms (Section II). Our experiments were performed on the Corel-1000 database, which is a generalist, complex database of natural images featuring various scenes and objects[2]. Corel-1000 contains exactly 1000 images organized as 10 classes with 100 images per class. In the second step, an ordering is performed inside each class of the reference image, based on a similarity measure, to provide the user with the most relevant images compared to the reference.

The following section of the paper explains the principle of image indexing based on weighted color histograms that are further used in the Mean-Shift method. The third section details the Mean-Shift method itself and how it is used to characterize objects in a sequence of images. It also presents an improvement of Mean-Shift by introducing Gaussian mixtures for the detection - or not - of objects among images featuring various scenes and objects. The fourth section presents the results of our work, and finally the fifth section concludes the paper. In the rest of paper we will denote our method WHMSGM for: "Weighted Histograms as input Mean-Shift and Gaussian Mixtures".

---

[2] Available at: http://wang.ist.psu.edu/docs/related.shtml

II.2 Color indexing

II.2.1 Weighted color histograms

Image indexing by color histograms consists in computing the statistical distribution of the colors in an image. For an image of size $M \times N$ pixels, the histogram $h(c)$ is formerly defined as:

$$h(c) = \frac{1}{MN} \sum_{i=0}^{M-1} \sum_{j=0}^{N-1} \delta(f(i,j) - c) \quad \forall c \in C \tag{1}$$

Where $f(i,j)$ is the color of the image f at pixel (i, j), c is a color varying in a colorset C, and δ is the Kronecker function:

$$\delta(x,y) = 1 \text{ If } x \text{ equals } y, 0 \text{ otherwise.} \tag{2}$$

However this approach is limited because it does not take into account the spatial distribution of colors inside the image. To overcome this issue, an efficient and simple way consists in weighting the histogram by the local color activity around each pixel [27]. Then (1) becomes:

$$h(c) = \frac{1}{MN} \sum_{i=0}^{M-1} \sum_{j=0}^{N-1} w(i,j) \delta(f(i,j) - c) \quad \forall c \in C \tag{3}$$

Where $w(i,j)$ is the coefficient associated to each pixel. A commonly used weighting is based on Laplacian, because it provides good information regarding uniform areas or edges:

$$w(i,j) = \Delta^2(i,j) \tag{4}$$

More generally, weight $w(i,j)$ has to be a statistical measure that takes into account the probability of the current color within its neighborhood. For example the inverse of entropy is commonly used too, since local entropy $E_{ij}(c)$ is null in a uniform neighborhood and maximal where there are no identical colors within a neighborhood:

$$w(i,j) = \frac{1}{E_{ij}(c)} \tag{5}$$

That is the weighting scheme we used in our implementation.

II.2.2   Color packets

Our work deals with databases of color images, where every color pixel is usually coded as a triplet (R, G, B) of values of red, green, and blue. Usually for general images, each color channel is discretized into 256 bins. This gives a choice of color among a range of $256^3 = 16,777,216$ possible colors. This is the number of colors in the colorset C in (1), (3), and (5). Computing a weighted histogram like in (3) with such a palette would be too much time consuming, especially in case of large databases containing hundreds or thousands of images, and of high resolution images. For example pictures from digital cameras are nowadays commonly over five million pixels. In order to reduce the computing time, the color set is split into color packets. A parameter p controls the number of packets, and thus the number of colors inside each packet. Table 1 shows the parameter p (first column), the number of colors in each packet (second column), and the number of color packets (third column).

Table II-1

THE PARAMETER P, THE NUMBER OF COLORS IN EACH PACKET, AND THE NUMBER OF COLOR PACKETS.

Parameter p	$2^{(p)}$ colors per packet	$2^{(24-p)}$ packets
0	1	16,777,216
3	8	2,097,152
6	64	262,144
9	512	32,768
12	4,096	4,096
15	32,768	512
18	262,144	64
21	2,097,152	8
24	16,777,216	1

In the indexing phase, (3) can be easily adapted to compute the frequencies $h(p_c)$ of color packets p_c instead of single colors c. The choice of parameter p depends on the compromise we want between computing time and accuracy of indexing.

An extreme case would be to consider $p=24$, meaning that the whole colorset is seen as a single packet containing all the colors in the image. It would be the worst case to distinguish between different images but the fastest for computing time. Another extreme case would be to set p=0, where a packet contains one single color, yielding maximum accuracy but at the cost of a much higher computing time. In our implementation we set p to 9. The next section explains how the weighted histogram of an image is used to compute 2D Gaussian kernels of color distributions.

II.3   Mean-Shift and Gaussian Mixtures

II.3.1   Mean-Shift

The Mean-Shift algorithm is a non parametric clustering technique which does not require prior knowledge of the number of clusters, and does not constrain the shape of the clusters.

Given n data points x_i, $i = 1,...,n$ on a d-dimensional space R^d, the multivariate kernel density estimate obtained with kernel $K(x)$ and window radius h is

$$f(x) = \frac{1}{nh^d} \sum_{i=1}^{n} K(\frac{x - x_i}{h})$$ (6)

Where K is defined as: $K(x) = c.k\left(\|x\|^2\right)$ with c a normalization constant which assures $K(x)$ integrates to 1.

The modes of the density function are located at the zeros of the gradient function $\nabla f(x) = 0$.

The gradient of the density estimator (6) is

$$\nabla f(x) = \frac{2c}{nh^{d+2}} \sum_{i+1}^{n} (x_i - x) g\left(\left\|\frac{x - x_i}{h}\right\|^2\right)$$

$$= \frac{2c}{nh^{d+2}} \left[\sum_{i+1}^{n} g\left(\left\|\frac{x - x_i}{h}\right\|^2\right)\right] \left[\frac{\sum_{i=1}^{n} x_i g\left(\left\|\frac{x - x_i}{h}\right\|^2\right)}{\sum_{i=1}^{n} g\left(\left\|\frac{x - x_i}{h}\right\|^2\right)} - x\right]$$ (7)

Where $g(s) = -k'(s)$.

The first term is proportional to the density estimate at x and the second term

$$m_h(x) = \frac{\sum_{i=1}^{n} x_i g\left(\left\|\frac{x-x_i}{h}\right\|^2\right)}{\sum_{i=1}^{n} g\left(\left\|\frac{x-x_i}{h}\right\|^2\right)} - x \tag{8}$$

is the Mean-Shift. The Mean-Shift vector always points toward the direction of the maximum increase in the density. The Mean-Shift procedure, obtained by successive

- Computation of the Mean-Shift vector $m_h(x^t)$,
- Translation of the window $x^{t+1} = x^t + m_h(x^t)$

is guaranteed to converge to a point where the gradient of density function is zero.

The method we developed consists in analyzing the colors of a « reference image », then building a confidence map by comparison to another image called « target image ». The confidence map is built by comparing the color distributions between the reference and the target images. Especially, we try to detect in the target image the objects characterized by their colors in the reference image, and then detect – or not – a confidence peak. This is how we adapted the Mean-Shift method to our purpose.

The comparison between two color distributions, technically in our case two weighted color histograms (see Section II), is performed by a statistical distance commonly called similarity measure. The classic Mean-Shift method used in object tracking in videos usually works with only one single class, i.e. one single 2D Gaussian distribution of colors to characterize the object to track. Our contribution here, taking into account the fact that some objects or scenes can be complex, is to introduce Gaussian mixtures [28] and then measure the similarity between a set of 2D Gaussian distributions that characterize the colors of a single object or scene. Gaussian mixtures are presented in the next section.

II.3.2 Gaussian Mixtures

Gaussian Mixtures are a widely used statistical tool in various fields like science, engineering and in particular computer science. It is used to modelize digital data as an instance of the clustering of a set of objects [29]. The modelization is computed as a weighted sum of M Gaussian probability density functions, commonly called Gaussian kernels, as expressed in (9).

$$P(x \mid \lambda) = \sum_{i=1}^{M} w_i g(x \mid \mu_i, \Sigma_i) \qquad (9)$$

$$g(x \mid \mu_i, \Sigma_i) = \frac{1}{(2\pi)^{D/2} |\Sigma_i|^{1/2}} \exp\left\{ -\frac{1}{2}(x - \mu_i) \sum_i^{-1} (x - \mu_i) \right\} \qquad (10)$$

$\lambda = \{w_i, \mu_i \Sigma_i\}, D = $Dimension, $w_i = $weight

The variance, mean, and amplitude of each Gaussian kernel have to be estimated. This can be done with maximum-likelihood estimation thanks to an iterative algorithm of expectance-maximization (EM) [30].

In our application, Gaussian Mixtures are used to characterize several classes of colors for a single object or scene in the reference image, then these Gaussian kernels are compared to those of different target images, in order to detect – or not – the same object or scene. The similarity measure use to compare several 2D Gaussian kernels between a pair of images is the Bhattacharyya distance [31,32,33]. The Bhattacharyya distance measures the similarity between two discrete or continuous probability distributions. It is closely related to the famous Bhattacharyya coefficient which measures the degree of overlapping between two statistical data sets.

II.4   Results and experiments

II.4.1   Image database

Our method was tested on the Corel-1000 image database, which is a subset of the Corel database. Corel is a collection of about 60,000 images, created by the research group of Professor Wang at the Penn State University. Corel-1000 is a subset of Corel organized in 10 categories of each 100 natural images. Corel-1000 is a challenging image database for computed CBIR due to the high variability of images inside a same category. The figure 1 presents a few images from Corel-1000. The official 10 classes of Corel-1000 are: Africa, Buildings, Mountains, Elephants, Dinosaurs, Beaches, Bus, Flowers, Food, and Horses.

Figure II-1. A few images from Corel-1000.

II.4.2 Confusion matrix

Table II-2
CONFUSION MATRIX (IN PERCENTAGES) FOR THE WHMSGM METHOD.

↓ True classes	Africa	Beaches	Buildings	Buses	Dinosaurs	Elephants	Flowers	Horses	Mountains	Food
Africa	44	3	27	3	0	16	0	2	3	2
Beaches	0	57	14	1	0	6	2	0	20	0
Buildings	1	29	34	3	0	2	0	0	31	0
Buses	18	2	4	67	0	0	1	2	5	1
Dinosaurs	6	0	2	8	69	5	0	1	3	6
Elephants	27	3	13	4	3	30	0	2	5	13
Flowers	11	0	1	24	2	0	30	5	0	27
Horses	12	6	11	6	0	8	0	50	4	3
Mountains	1	27	7	8	0	5	0	0	52	0
Food	23	0	3	15	0	3	2	2	0	52

To test our WHMSGM method, a reference image was randomly picked-up in each category, so ten reference images in total, and built a confusion matrix of the results. A confusion matrix is a simple tool used to measure the quality of a classification system. Each column of the matrix represents the number of occurrences of an estimated class, while each row represents the number of occurrences of a reference class. Thus a confusion matrix shows directly how accurate a classification system performs.

The confusion matrix obtained by our method is given in table 2, where we can see that the diagonal values are very good classification rates for most of the reference images, especially for classes Dinosaurs (69%) and Bus (67%). The lowest rates obtained for Elephants and Flowers classes (30%) are explained by the fact that the scenes and objects of these two categories are highly shared with other classes. For instance, many images from the Elephants category have been classified as belonging to the Africa one

(27%), which is not an abnormal result considering the colors and tones (variations of brown) in the images of these two categories.

II.4.3   Intra-class ordering

Classification of each reference image thanks to the confusion matrix as explained in the previous section, we perform what we call an intra-class ordering of the images of each category, by relevance, or similarity, to the reference image picked up into that category. Our method orders the images in each category from the most similar, according to the Bhattacharyya distance (see Section III. B.), to the less similar to the reference image. The figure 2 shows the reference images randomly chosen in each category. The figure 3 shows the results of the intra-class ordering for each of the reference images of the figure 2. The percentage under each image represents the similarity measure between the reference image of the category and the current image.

Figure II-2. Reference images.

Reference images

%99.43 %92.04 %92.66 %92.21 %100.00

%99.09 %91.33 %90.95 %89.99 %100.00

%98.37 %89.26 %90.24 %89.18 %100.00

%98.04 %87.82 %89.40 %88.69 %100.00

%98.03 %87.15 %88.71 %88.33 %100.00

%98.00 %85.89 %87.21 %88.05 %100.00

%97.64 %85.34 %87.17 %87.75 %99.96

%97.48 %85.13 %86.70 %87.69 %99.95

Figure II-3. Intra-class ordering for the reference images shown in figure 2.

II.5 Conclusion

As a conclusion, the authors think that this work contributes to the domain of Content-Based Color Image Retrieval. Our content descriptor is the color distribution of images, computed as weighted color histograms. These color histograms are then modelized as a set of 2D Gaussian kernels, thanks to the combination of the Mean-Shift analysis method and the Gaussian mixtures technique.

Our results on a complex database or natural images (Corel-1000), containing various scenes and objects, show that the developed tool could be used as an automatic color image search engine. If extended to other image databases, the user could be provided with similar images to an image he chooses or uploads as a reference to the engine.

In the near future, this work should be enhanced with other research in the same field, especially considering the combination of several low-level descriptors like colors, feature points and edges.

Conclusion générale

Cette thèse de maîtrise s'inscrit dans la catégorie « recherche des images par le contenu et classification » en utilisant l'approche statistique « Mean-Shift ». Cette approche simple et efficace a été développée et améliorée grâce aux avancées des travaux aux cours des dernières années sur l'extraction de caractéristiques globales des images et des techniques d'analyse des données. Dans notre travail, l'indexation d'une image se fait à partir de sa représentation par histogrammes de couleurs.

Le travail présenté dans cette thèse met en avant l'importance et l'efficacité de l'indexation, de la recherche et de la classification des images à l'aide de l'approche statistique « Mean-Shift ». Beaucoup de temps a été consacré à étudier les techniques de classification et de suivi d'objets dans les images pour en arriver au choix de cette approche.

Plusieurs lectures bibliographiques nous ont permis de constater que l'indexation textuelle ne garantit pas une indexation efficace des images. Pour remédier à ces limites, nous avons proposé le modèle « Mean-Shift » adapté aux histogrammes de couleurs d'images numériques pour une recherche par le contenu plus performante.

La classification et l'ordonnancement d'images a fait l'objet de la deuxième phase de cette recherche. Son objectif était de trouver le modèle de classification le mieux adapté à la méthode d'indexation proposée pour une base d'images plus complexe que celle utilisée dans la première recherche, tout en évitant les problèmes dus aux données volumineuses et de grande dimension. Dans ce sens, nous avons adopté une catégorisation de toute la base d'images en plusieurs classes, pour chacune desquelles nous avons appliqué la méthode d'analyse « Mean-Shift ». Nous avons expérimentalement fait varier le nombre de classes jusqu'à ce qu'on arrive aux résultats optimaux et aux similitudes les plus significatives. Ensuite, un ordonnancement intra-classe a été effectué pour chaque catégorie, allant de l'image la plus similaire à l'image requête, à celle ayant le pourcentage de similarité le plus faible.

Les extensions et les améliorations possibles à l'approche étudiée sont nombreuses. L'une d'entre elles consiste à fusionner d'autres descripteurs aux histogrammes de couleurs pour mieux caractériser les images. En effet, la combinaison d'autres informations, telles que la texture, les points caractéristiques, ou les moments de couleurs serait une piste intéressante pour traiter des bases d'images plus complexe et plus volumineuses. Également, nous comptons améliorer le temps de calcul en générant des fichiers exécutables rapides à partir d'un langage performant tel que le C ou le C++, codé et compilé de façon optimisée, en particulier au niveau des fonctions critiques.

BIBLIOGRAPHIE

[1] M. J. Swain and D. H. Ballard, "Color Indexing," International Journal of Computer Vision, pp. 11-32, 1991.

[2] P. Howarth and S. Rueger, "Evaluation of texture features for content-based image retrieval," Proceedings of the international conference on image and video retrieval N°3, pp. 326-334, 2004.

[3] P. Howarth, A. Yavlinsky, D. Heesch, and S. Rüger, "Visual features for content-based medical image retrieval," Notebook of the Cross Language Evaluation Forum (CLEF) Workshop, 2004.

[4] M. J. Swain and D. H. Ballard, "Color Indexing", International Journal of Computer Vision, pp. 11-32, 1991.

[5] J. Ohm, F. Bunjamin, W. Liebsch, B. Makai, K. Müller, B. Saberdest, and D. Zier, "A Visual Search Engine for Distributed Image and Video Database Retrieval Applications", Proceedings of the Third International Conference on Visual Information and Information Systems, pp. 187-194, 1999.

[6] M. Stricker and M. Orengo, "Similarity of color images", Proceedings of SPIE Vol. 2, Storage and Retrieval for Image and Video Databases, pp. 381-392, 1995.

[7] D. G. Lowe, "Object Recognition from Local Scale-Invariant Features", Proceedings of the International Conference on Computer Vision, Vol. 2, pp. 1150-1157, 1999.

[8] D. G. Lowe, "Distinctive Image Features from Scale-Invariant Keypoints", The International Journal of Computer Vision, pp. 91-110, 2004.

[9] Z. Zivkovic and B. Kröse, "An EM-like algorithm for color-histogram-based object tracking", IEEE Conference on Computer Vision and Pattern Recognition, Vol. 1, pp. 798-803, 2004.

[10]   D. Comaniciu, "Mean Shift: A Robust Approch Toward Feature Space Analysis", IEEE Transactions on Pattern Analysis and Machine Intelligence, Vol. 24, No. 5, 2002.

[11]   N. Boujemaa, S. Boughorbel, and C. Vertan, "Soft Color Signatures for Image Retrieval by Content", European Society for Fuzzy Logic and Technology (EUSFLAT), pp. 394-401, 2001.

[12]   T. Kanungo, D. M. Mount, N. S. Netanyahu, C. D. Piatko, R. Silverman, A. Y. Wu, "An efficient k-means clustering algorithm: Analysis and implementation". IEEE Trans. Pattern Analysis and Machine Intelligence, Vol. 24, pp. 881–892, 2009.

[13]   F. Nielsen and S. Boltz, « The Burbea-Rao and Bhattacharyya centroids », ArXiv:1004.5049v1, 2010.

[14]   A. Bhattacharyya, "On a Measure of Divergence Between Two Statistical Populations Defined by their Probability Distributions", Bull. Calcutta Math. Soc., Vol. 35, pp. 99-110, 1943.

[15]   T.Kailath ,« The Divergence and Bhattacharyya Distance Measures in Signal Selection », IEEE Transactions on Communication Technology, Vol. 15, No. 1, pp. 52–60, 1967.

[16]   J. Sivic and A. Zisserman, Video Google: "A Text Retrieval Approach to Object Matching in Videos", Proceedings of the Ninth IEEE International Conference on Computer Vision, Vol. 2, pp. 1470-1477, 2003.

[17]   W. Zhao, Y. Jiang, and C. Ngo, "Keyframe retrieval by keypoints: Can point-to-point matching help?", Proceedings of the 5th international Conference on Image and Video Retrieval, pp. 72-81, 2006.

[18]   S. Newsam and Y. Yang, "Comparing Global and Interest Point Descriptors for Similarity Retrieval in Remote Sensed Imagery", Proceedings of the 15th International Symposium on Advances in Geographic Information Systems, 2007.

[19]   W. Bouachir, M. Kardouchi, and N. Belacel, "Improving Bag of Visual Words Image Retrieval: A Fuzzy Weighting Scheme for Efficient Indexation", Fifth International Conference on Signal Image Technology and Internet Based Systems, pp. 215-220, 2009.

[20]   M. J. Swain and D. H. Ballard, "Color Indexing", International Journal of Computer Vision, pp. 11-32, 1991.

[21]   J. Ohm, F. Bunjamin, W. Liebsch, B. Makai, K. Müller, B. Saberdest and D. Zier, "A Visual Search Engine for Distributed Image and Video Database Retrieval Applications", Proceedings of the Third International Conference on Visual Information and Information Systems, pp. 187-194, 1999.

[22]   M. Stricker and M. Orengo, "Similarity of color images", Proceedings of SPIE Vol. 2, Storage and Retrieval for Image and Video Databases, pp. 381-392, 1995.

[23]   D. G. Lowe, "Object Recognition from Local Scale-Invariant Features", Proceedings of the International Conference on Computer Vision, Vol. 2, pp. 1150-1157, 1999.

[24]   D. G. Lowe, "Distinctive Image Features from Scale-Invariant Keypoints", The International Journal of Computer Vision, pp. 91-110, 2004.

[25]   Z. Zivkovic and B. Kröse, "An EM-like algorithm for color-histogram-based object tracking", IEEE Conference on Computer Vision and Pattern Recognition, Vol. 1, pp. 798-803, 2004.

[26]   D. Comaniciu, "Mean Shift: A Robust Approch Toward Feature Space Analysis",IEEE Transactions on pattern analysis and machine intelligence, Vol. 24, No. 5, 2002.

[27]   N. Boujemaa, S. Boughorbel, and C. Vertan, "Soft Color Signatures for Image Retrieval by Content", European Society for Fuzzy Logic and Technology (EUSFLAT), pp. 394-401, 2001.

[28]   P. Bruneau, « De l'utilisation pratique des mélanges de gaussiennes », Journée des doctorants de l'Ecole Doctorale STIM (JDOC'09), Nantes (France), Avril 2009.

[29]   C. M. Bishop, "Pattern Recognition and Machine Learning", Chapter 9, pp. 424–444, Springer, 2006.

[30]   A. P. Dempster, N. M. Laird, and D. B. Rubin, "Maximum likelihood from incomplete data via the EM algorithm", Journal of the Royal Statistical Society - B Series, B(39), pp. 1–38, 1977.

[31]   F. Nielsen and S. Boltz, « The Burbea-Rao and Bhattacharyya centroids », ArXiv:1004.5049v1, 2010

[32]   A. Bhattacharyya, "On a Measure of Divergence Between Two Statistical Populations Defined by their Probability Distributions", Bull. Calcutta Math. Soc., Vol. 35, pp. 99-110, 1943.

[33]   T. Kailath , « The Divergence and Bhattacharyya Distance Measures in Signal Selection », IEEE Transactions on Communication Technology, Vol. 15, No. 1, pp. 52–60, 1967.

www.ingramcontent.com/pod-product-compliance
Lightning Source LLC
LaVergne TN
LVHW042351060326
832902LV00006B/530